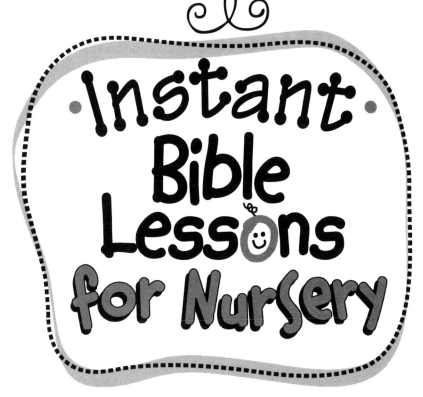

Give Thanks to God

Mary J. Davis

These pages may be copied.
Permission is granted to the buyer of this book to
photocopy student materials for use with
Sunday school or Bible teaching classes.

For information regarding the CPSIA on this printed material call:
203-595-3636 and provide reference # LANC-473236

rainbowpublishers®

Rainbow Publishers • P.O. Box 261129 • San Diego, CA 92196
www.RainbowPublishers.com

With thanks to all those volunteers I have been privileged to work with throughout the years. You have blessed my life in many ways, and I thank God for you.

Instant Bible Lessons for Nursery: Give Thanks to God
©2013 by Rainbow Publishers, second printing
ISBN 10: 1-58411-119-4
ISBN 13: 978-1-58411-119-1
Rainbow reorder# RB38711
RELIGION / Christian Ministry / Children

Rainbow Publishers
P.O. Box 261129
San Diego, CA 92196
www.RainbowPublishers.com

Cover Illustrator: Stacey Lamb
Interior Illustrator: Jon Mitchell

Scriptures are from the *Holy Bible: New International Version* (North American Edition), ©1973, 1978, 1984 by the International Bible Society. Used by permission of Zondervan Bible Publishers.

Permission is granted to the buyer of this book to photocopy student materials for use with Sunday school or Bible teaching classes.

All rights reserved. Except as noted above, no part of this publication may be reproduced, stored in a retrieval system, or transmitted in any form or by any means without written permission of Rainbow Publishers.

Printed in the United States of America

Contents

Introduction 5
   How to Use This Book 5

Chapter 1: Thank You God for My Family 7
Story to Share 7
Story Poster 9
Families Song 10
I Love You Sign Language Rhyme 11
Family Picture Frame 12
Family Prayer Glove 13
My Family Bulletin Board 14
Cookie Match Puzzle 15
Family Play Figures 16

Chapter 2: Thank You God for My Friends 17
Story to Share 17
Story Poster 18
Friends Song 20
Come on Down Rhyme 21
Friends Room Garland 22
Friendship Coloring Mats 23
Wobble Friends 24
Zacchaeus Easy Dot Puzzle 25
The Best Friend Ever 26

Chapter 3: Thank You God for My Home 27
Story to Share 27
Story Poster 28
Simple Playhouse 30
Things in My Home Puzzle 31
Let's Build a Home 32
My Home Book 34

Chapter 4: Thank You God for My Pets 37
Story to Share 37
Story Poster 38
Pet Food Puzzle 40
Pets Song 41
Peek-a-Boo Pets 42
Indoor/Outdoor Pets Book 43
Pet Parade 46
Hiding Lamb 47

Chapter 5: Thank You God for Food 49
Story to Share 49
Story Poster 50
Large Matching Game 52
Thank You Bibs 54
God Gave Us Good Food Song 56
Thanking God Action Rhyme 57
Praying Hands Plaque 58
Praying Hands Puzzle 59

Chapter 6: Thank You God for Water 61
Story to Share 61
Story Poster 62
God Gives Us Water Action Rhyme 64
Thankful for Water Cup 65
Water Rhymes Booklet 66
Water Wheel Game 67
Things We Do with Water Puzzle 68
Water Shakers 69

Chapter 7: Thank You God for Clothes 71
Story to Share 71
Story Poster 72

Play Clothes Paper Doll 74
What Shall I Wear? Song.................................76
Coat of Many Colors Mobile 77
My Clothes Puzzle 78
Mosaic Verse Poster 79
Story in a Diaper Bag 80

Chapter 8: Thank You God for My Church 81
Story to Share...81
Story Poster..82
Offering Tray Game..84
My Church Song 85
I Can Make a Church Action Rhyme 86
Sharing Bank..87
Meet Together With Gladness Puzzle...............88

Chapter 9: More Give Thanks to God Activities 89
Clapping Rhyme 89
Thank You Praying Toy....................................90
Glow in the Dark Praying Hands Plaque 91
Beanbag Toss Game..92
Praying Hands..95
Rattling Roller Game 96

Introduction

Babies are in the nursery room week after week. Nursery workers hold, rock, feed and change babies' diapers. Now you can turn routine activities into teachable moments. Each and every week, volunteers have dozens of opportunities to help instill God's Word and His love in the lives of even the youngest children.

The lessons in *Instant Bible Lessons for Nursery: Give Thanks to God* include Bible stories about familiar things a young child can be thankful for, such as family, food, pets and clothes. Teachers can tell Bible stories, say the memory verse and present activities that will appeal to a variety of nursery-aged children. If your nursery has only babies one week, use the story poster ideas and sing the verse songs many times during class. Older babies will enjoy the crafts and touchable activities. Some of the crafts and games may seem a little old for babies, but the children will enjoy "helping" as much as they can. All the while, the teacher can repeat the story and memory verses for great one-on-one activities.

You may send story posters, song/rhyme pages and many other activities from this book home with parents so they may continue the lesson theme throughout the week.

Get ready to have fun in the nursery!

✶ How to Use This Book ✶

Each chapter begins with a Bible story which you may read to your class or to a child one-on-one. The questions after each lesson can be used as an opportunity for you to continue telling the story. Ask and answer each question for the children. Encourage older babies to repeat some of the words of the story or memory verse with you.

Every chapter includes a bulletin board story poster with the memory verse and suggestions for using the poster as an activity. All activities are tagged with one of the icons below, so you can quickly flip through the chapter and select the projects you need. Simply cut off the teacher instructions on the pages and duplicate.

Chapter 1
Thank You God for My Family

Memory Verse

[Abraham's]... son Isaac was born to him.
~Genesis 21:5

 Story to Share

Abraham and Sarah were very old. They both loved God very much. But Abraham and Sarah wanted something very much. They wanted a baby of their own. They wanted to have a family.

God promised Abraham that Sarah would have a baby. God kept his promise. Soon, Sarah had a little baby boy. His name was Isaac. Abraham and Sarah thanked God for their new little baby.

~Based on Genesis 12:1-3

Story Review

1. What did Abraham and Sarah want to have? They wanted to have a child of their own. They wanted to have a family.
2. What did God promise Abraham? God promised Abraham that Sarah would have a baby.
3. What did Abraham and Sarah name their baby? They named their little boy Isaac.

Parent Corner

1. Make a Bible lessons book to share with your child. Place eight plastic page protectors inside a clean three-ring binder. Decorate the front of the binder by taping your baby's picture onto it. Write with permanent marker, *[name]'s Bible Story Book*. Slip the take-home paper from each lesson inside a page protector. Look at the book together while you tell each story to your baby.

2. Show your baby pictures of your family. Say each person's name. Help the child fold his/her hands while you say, **We give thanks to God for Emma. We give thanks to God for Mommy and Daddy. We give thanks to God for Jack.**

3. When the family gathers for dinner, have everyone hold hands. Help your baby point to each person while you say, **We thank God that Rachel is part of our family. We give thanks to God for our families.**

Bulletin Board

What You Need
- pattern on page 9
- clear adhesive-backed plastic
- magazine pictures of families
- glue

What To Do
1. Depending on how you want to use the poster (see ideas below), enlarge, reduce or simply copy page 9 to fit your bulletin board space.
2. To use the poster as an in-class activity, turn the poster over and help the children glue a picture of a "today" family to the back of the poster. Write, "Thank you God for my family."

My Family

Story Poster

Poster Pointer

Reduce the size of poster to about one-half. Cover both sides of poster with clear adhesive-backed plastic. Use scissors to round off sharp corners. Let each child hold a storybook while you tell the story.

Song

What You Need
- duplicated page
- crayons

What To Do
1. Sing the song "Families", to the tune of "Deep and Wide."
2. Sing more verses using the extra verse phrases.

Families Song

Families

Families

God gave us families to love.

Families

Families

God gave us families to love.

⟶ Extra verses:

Substitute any of these words for "families": Mommies, Daddies, Brothers, Sisters, Grandmas, Grandpas.

I Love You Sign Language Rhyme

Rhyme

What You Need
- duplicated page

What To Do
1. Say the rhyme with the children using the simple signs.
2. Help older babies make the signs.

Love
[cross hands over heart]

Love
[cross hands over heart]

God gave us families
[point to God]

To Love
[cross hands over heart]

My Family

Family Picture Frame

Easy Craft

What You Need
- page duplicated to card stock for each child
- scissors
- crayons

What To Do
1. Before class, cut the opening from the front of the frame.
2. Fold page in half to form a picture frame.
3. Help older babies scribble-color their picture frames.
4. Send a frame home with each child.

My Family

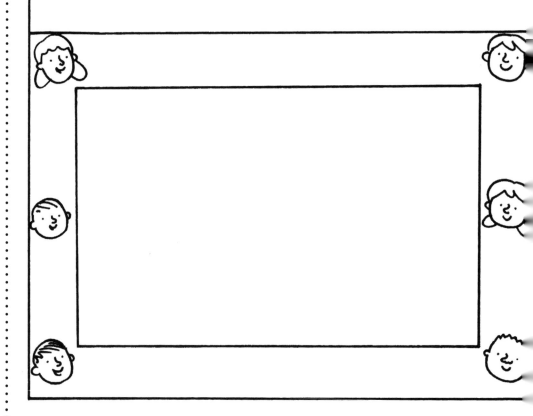

Family Prayer Glove

Learning Play

What You Need
- duplicated page
- an old glove
- scissors
- tape or glue

What To Do
1. Before class, cut the five family figures from the pattern page. Glue one figure to the end of each of the five fingers on the palm side of the glove.
2. Use one-on-one with each baby or with a group of children. Wear the glove. Let each child touch the figures on the prayer glove.
3. Say, **This is Mommy. Let's pray and thank God for Mommy. Thank you God for giving me a special Mommy.** Repeat with each family figure.

My Family

Bulletin Board

What You Need
- duplicated page
- instant camera and film
- tape

What To Do
1. Before class, cut out the rectangles from the pattern page, one per child. You might want to call or write each family and ask the entire family to come into the nursery before class time this week.
2. Take an instant photo of each baby with his/her family.
3. Fasten each photo to the "We give thanks" rectangles. Write the baby's name in the blank on the rectangle.
4. Fasten the finished "thank you" pictures to the bulletin board.
5. Carry the children often to the bulletin board. Say, **This is Zack's family. Thank you God for Zack's family.**

My Family

My Family Bulletin Board

We give thanks to God for

_____'s family

Cookie Match Game

Hands On

What You Need
- duplicated page
- clear adhesive-backed plastic
- Vanilla wafer-sized round cookies, three per child
- gel icing

What To Do
1. Before class, cover the pattern page with adhesive-backed plastic.
2. Help the children place a cookie on each of the Mom, Dad, and baby face circles.
3. Squeeze some gel icing onto each cookie to make eyes and a big smile.
4. Say, **The Mommy is happy. She is thankful for her family.** Repeat phrases for each member of the family.

My Family

Hands-On

What You Need
- duplicated page
- clean dish soap bottles, lids removed
- scissors
- glue

What To Do
1. Before class, cut out the Mommy, Daddy and baby from the pattern page. Glue each figure to a soap bottle.
2. Let each baby hold the bottles, stand them on a table, move them around, or whatever they wish.
3. Say, **This is Jeni. Here is Jeni's Mom. Thank you God for Jeni's family.**

My Family

Family Play Figures

Chapter 2
Thank You God for My Friends

Memory Verse

Jesus said, "Zacchaeus, come down."
~Luke 19:5

Story to Share

Zacchaeus heard people talking about Jesus a lot. He wondered, "What would it be like to have a wonderful friend like Jesus?"

Well, one day, Zacchaeus heard people shouting, "Jesus is coming to town! Jesus is coming to town!"

Zacchaeus hurried to where the crowd was gathering. Zacchaeus wanted to see Jesus. But, Zacchaeus was too short. He couldn't see over all the people. He stood on his tippy toes and tried to see Jesus. He tried to jump up high to see Jesus. He tried to squeeze through the crowd to see Jesus. But he just could not see Jesus.

Zacchaeus said, "I'll climb this tree." Zacchaeus climbed a tree. He saw Jesus coming closer and closer.

Jesus stopped right under that tree. "Zacchaeus," Jesus said. "Come down from that tree. I want to go to your house."

Zacchaeus hurried right down from the tree. He took Jesus to his house. Zacchaeus was very happy that Jesus was his friend.

~Based on Luke 19:1-10

Story Review

1. Who wanted to see Jesus? Zacchaeus wanted to see Jesus.
2. What did Zacchaeus do when he couldn't see Jesus? Zacchaeus climbed a tree.
3. Who became Zacchaeus' friend that day? Jesus became Zacchaeus' friend.

Parent Corner

1. *Read to Me time.* Hold your baby on your lap while sitting in your favorite story-time chair. Open your Bible or picture Bible to the story of creation and read the story.
2. Schedule a play date with another baby around the same age as your child. Even if both babies are very young, say often, **Thank you God for my friends.**

Bulletin Board

What You Need
- pattern on page 19
- clear adhesive-backed plastic
- heart stickers

What To Do
1. Depending on how you want to use the poster (see ideas below), enlarge, reduce, or simply copy page 19 to fit your bulletin board space.
2. To make a take-home paper, duplicate the story page to the back of story poster.
3. To use the poster as an in-class activity, help the baby stick some heart stickers onto the poster page. Say, **We love our friends. Thank you God for our friends.**
4. Older babies will enjoy scribble-coloring the poster page.

My Friends

Story Poster

Poster Pointer

Cover the front and back sides of story poster with clear adhesive-backed plastic. Trim corners so they aren't pointed. Place the covered picture on high chair trays or on the table where you will be holding babies for feeding time, story time or playtime. Tell the story or say the memory verse while the children are playing with the poster. Older babies may enjoy scribble-coloring on the covered posters. The posters can then be wiped off and used again. Use as a place mat on high chairs or at the table where the teacher or helpers hold children for story or snack time.

🎵 Song

What You Need
- duplicated page

What To Do
1. Sing the song "Friends," to the tune of "The Itsy Bitsy Spider."
2. Sing the song again, helping children hug themselves every time you sing the word "friend."

Friends Song

Jesus was a friend to Zacchaeus
And He is a friend to me.

I can be friend to others like Jesus
wants me to be.

Thank you God for all the friends,
you have given to me.

I am thankful for my friends,
like Jesus wants me to be.

My Friends

Come On Down Rhyme

"Come on down."
[wave arm toward self]

"Come on down."
[wave arm toward self]

Jesus told Zacchaeus,
[cup hands around mouth]

"Come on down!"
[wave arm toward self]

"I will be your friend."
[wave arm toward self]

"I will be your friend."
[wave arm toward self]

Jesus told Zacchaeus,
[cup hands around mouth]

"I will be your friend!"
[hug self]

Rhyme

What You Need
- duplicated page

What To Do
1. Say the rhyme and do the actions.
2. Say the rhyme again, and help children do the actions.

My Friends

Friends Room Garland

Room Decoration

What You Need
- This page, duplicated.
- construction paper
- glue
- yarn
- crayons
- tape

What To Do
1. Before class, cut out a boy banner for each boy and a girl banner for each girl in your nursery.
2. Glue each banner onto brightly colored construction paper.
3. Write a child's name on each banner. Let them scribble-color on the banners if desired.
5. Fasten each banner together by taping a length of yarn between each to form a garland.
6. Hang the garland across a bulletin board or wall space.
7. Carry children to the garland often during class. Say, **This is Abby. Abby is our friend. Thank you God for friends.**

My Friends

Give thanks to God

for friends

Give thanks to God

for friends

Friendship Coloring Mats

Learning Play

What You Need
- duplicated page, one copy for every two or three children
- crayons
- construction paper
- tape

What To Do
1. Before class duplicate copies of this page and tape each to a larger piece of construction paper.
2. Place two or three babies at a table or on a play mat.
3. Help babies scribble-color the picture on the coloring mats. Have two or three babies work together.
4. Say, **Josh, Dylan and Chrissy are coloring together just like the children in our picture. What good friends we are. Thank you God for friends.**

My Friends

Wobble Friends

Easy Craft

What You Need
- duplicated page for each child
- large plastic Easter egg, one for each child
- scissors
- animal crackers
- tape
- crayons

What To Do
1. Before class, place animal crackers inside each egg and tape shut.
2. Cut out a "friends" strip for each child.
3. Help older babies scribble-color the "friends" strip.
4. Place the strip around the middle of the two caps. Tape the edge. Tape securely around all edges of the paper strip.
5. Show babies how to make the "friends" toy wobble.
6. Say, **God gives us friends. We give thanks to God for friends.**

My Friends

finished craft

* Zacchaeus *
Easy Dot Puzzle

Puzzle

What You Need
- duplicated page for each child
- crayons

What To Do
1. Help older babies hold a crayon and connect the dots to finish the tree.
2. Let babies scribble-color the picture while you retell the story of Zacchaeus.

My Friends

The Best Friend Ever

Easy Craft

What You Need
- page 26 duplicated to card stock for each child
- fruit roll-ups
- gel icing in tubes (to use for glue)
- yarn
- tape
- crayons

What To Do
1. Allow older babies to scribble-color their pictures of Jesus.
2. Tear strips of fruit roll-ups to fit along the top, bottom, and sides of picture.
3. Use gel icing like glue to stick the fruit roll-up strips around the edge of the picture, like a frame.
4. Tape a loop of yarn to the top of each picture for a hanger.

My Friends

Jesus, the Best Friend Ever!

Chapter 3
Thank You God for My Home

Memory Verse

Where you go I will go, and where you stay I will stay.
~Ruth 1:16

Story to Share

Naomi had two sons. Both sons died. Suddenly, Naomi didn't have any sons. She decided to go back to the home where she grew up. Naomi told her sons' wives to go back to their people.

Ruth said, "No, I will go where you go and make my home with you."

Ruth and Naomi went back to the land where Naomi lived long ago. Ruth took care of Naomi.

God blessed Ruth for coming far away from her home to help Naomi. Soon, a man named Boaz asked Ruth to marry him. Ruth had a new husband. Ruth and Naomi now had a new home with Boaz.

Naomi thanked God for her new home.

~Based on The Book of Ruth

Story Review

1. Who went with Naomi to a far-away home? Ruth went with Naomi to a far-away home.
2. How did God bless Ruth for taking care of Naomi? God gave Ruth a new husband and a new home.

Parent Corner

1. *In the car.* Tell the Bible story while riding in the car. The sound of your voice will sooth a fussy baby or keep the child entertained. Say or sing the memory verse or story theme in a fun way. Any tune will work. The child will begin to try to sing along with you and God's Word will be instilled in your baby's memory.

2. Carry your baby around your home. Say, **This is our kitchen where Mommy prepares our food. We give thanks to God for our home.** Say similar phrases for each room in the house.

3. Look at a home catalog or magazine with your baby. Point at the pictures of homes and say, **This is a pretty home. We thank God for our home.**

Bulletin Board

What You Need
- poster on page 29
- clear adhesive-backed plastic
- construction paper
- tape

What To Do
1. Depending on how you want to use the poster (see ideas below), enlarge, reduce or simply copy page 29 to fit your bulletin board space.
2. To make a take-home paper, duplicate the story page to the back of story poster.
3. To use the poster as an in-class activity, cut a triangle-shape for a roof from construction paper for each child. Help the children tape the roof to the top of the poster. Say, **Homes in Bible-times had a flat roof. We will make this home look like our homes today with a pointed roof. We give thanks to God for our homes.**

My Home

Story Poster

▭▭▷ Poster Pointer

Fasten a poster on the wall above the diaper station/changing table. Put another poster on a table close to the rocking chair. Use posters for one-on-one time with babies. Tell the Bible story or say the memory verse many times during nursery time.

Home Songs

Song

What You Need
- duplicated page

What To Do
1. Sing the "Thank You for My Home" song to the tune of "Row your Boat."
2. You may also sing the "God Gave Me a Home," song, to the tune of "Farmer in the Dell."

Thank you for my home,
For my happy home.
God gave me a happy home.
Thank you for my home.

God gave me a home
God gave me a home
I live there with my family
God gave me a home.

My Home

Things in My Home Puzzle

Puzzle

What You Need
- duplicated page
- crayons

What To Do
1. Show children the page. Say, **These are things we might have in our home.**
2. Have the child choose an item to color. Say, **James has a chair in his home. We give thanks to God for our homes.**
3. Older babies will enjoy scribble-coloring the page. Younger babies can look at the page while you point out each item and thank God for our homes.

My Home

Learning Play

What You Need
- pages 32 and 33, duplicated
- 4 pudding or gelatin boxes with lids intact
- scissors
- glue

What To Do
1. Before class, cut the four home sections from the pattern pages. Glue each section onto the front of a pudding or gelatin box. Tape the lids of the boxes closed. Tape all paper edges securely.
2. Help each baby lay the four boxes in order on a table or play mat to form a house.
3. Older babies will enjoy stacking the boxes upright to build a house.
4. Say, **We can build a home. We give thanks to God for our homes.**

My Home

Let's Build a Home

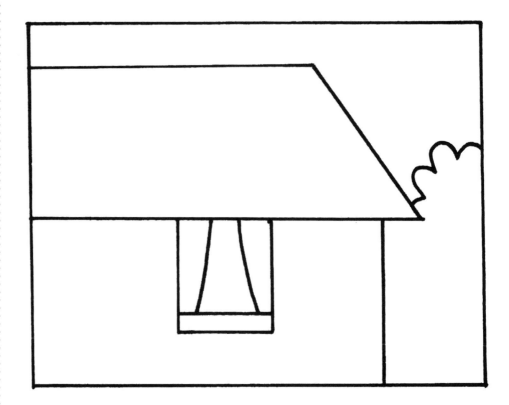

finished craft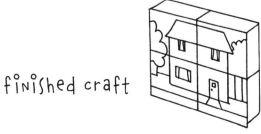

Read to Me

What You Need
- pages 34, 35 and 36, duplicated
- construction paper
- hole punch
- plastic rings (3)
- glue

What To Do
1. Before class, cut and glue each illustration to its own piece of construction paper.
2. Punch 3 holes through all layers of the book at the left edge. Fasten three plastic rings through the holes to hold the book together.
3. Hold each baby on your lap. Turn the pages as you read the book to the children. Babies love repetition and the soothing sound of your voice. This is a good one-on-one activity.

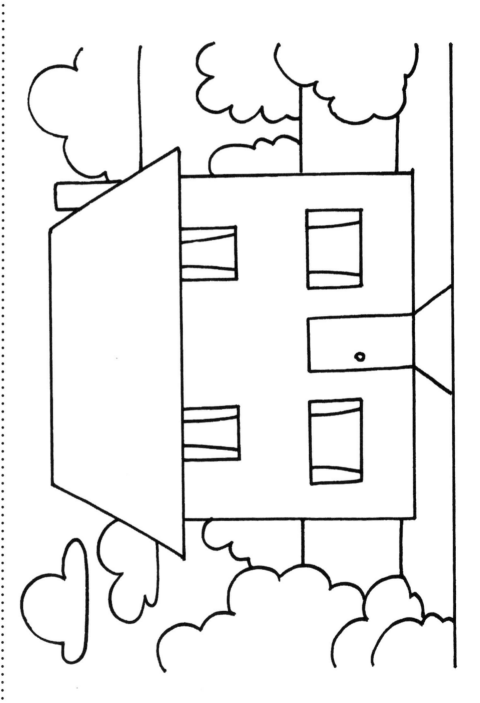

My Home

My home has a kitchen
Where Mom and Dad cook our food.
Then we sit at a table
To eat things that are good.

My home has a living room
Where we gather each day.
Sometimes we watch TV
And sometimes we play.

My home has a bedroom
That is just for me.
My special bed, my dresser
My clothes and my bear Mr. B.

My home has lots of rooms
For my family.
I thank God for the home
That He gave to me.

Chapter 4
Thank You God for My Pets

Memory Verse

I have found my lost sheep.
~Luke 15:6

Story to Share

Jesus told a story about a man who had many sheep. One day, the man counted his sheep. One sheep was not there.

The man left all his other sheep while he went to look for the lost one. He looked everywhere for his sheep.

Then he found the sheep. He was so happy to find his lost sheep. He said to all his friends, "Come to my house. We will celebrate and be happy that I have found my lost sheep."

Jesus wanted us to know that He loves each of us just like a little lost sheep. He would look for us everywhere, if we were lost. Jesus wants us to stay close to Him.

~Based on Luke 15:3-7

Story Review

1. How many sheep were lost? Just one sheep was lost.
2. What did the man do? He left all his sheep to go find the lost one.

Parent Corner

1. Fasten the story poster to the front of your refrigerator or another common place in the home. Every time you carry your baby close to the poster, retell the story. Let them touch the poster while you talk.
2. Gather stuffed animals that would be good pets, and place them in a basket. Help your baby take the animals out of the basket and put them into a second basket. Say, **What a pretty kitty. We give thanks to God for our pets.**
3. Let each baby hold a toy lamb. Retell the Bible story. Say, **Let's hug our little lamb. The man was happy when he found his lost little lamb.**

Bulletin Board

What You Need
- pattern on page 39
- clear adhesive-backed plastic
- whipped topping
- clean-up cloths

What To Do
1. Depending on how you want to use the poster (see ideas below), enlarge, reduce or simply copy page 39 to fit your bulletin board space.
2. To make a take-home paper, duplicate the story page to the back of story poster.
3. To use the poster as an in-class activity, let the babies spread whipped topping on the lamb (you may cover the poster with clear adhesive-backed plastic first if you wish).

My Pets

Story Poster

Poster Pointer

Reduce the size of the poster to fit onto the sides of plastic baby wipe containers. Glue or tape securely, one poster picture to at least one side of the containers. Make at least three or four blocks, or make one block with poster picture from each of the eight stories in this book. Help each baby stack the blocks. Point to the poster picture for the current lesson and retell the story, or say the memory verse with the children.

Puzzle

What You Need
- duplicated page
- crayons

What To Do
1. Help each baby trace dashed lines from each pet to its food.
2. Older babies will enjoy scribble-coloring the picture.
3. Say the name of each animal and discuss how we feed each, as well as the type of food we give each one. Say, **Pet birds live in a cage. We put bird seed in a little feeding cup inside the cage. It's fun to take care of our pets. We give thanks to God for our pets.**

My Pets

Pet Food Puzzle

40

Pets Song

God gave us our pets to love
Thank you, thank you, God.
My favorite pet is my dog.
Thank you, thank you, God.

With a woof woof here
And a woof woof there
Here a woof
There a woof
Everywhere a woof woof
God gave us our pets to love
Thank you, thank you, God.

⟶ Extra verses:

Cat: meow meow   Bird: chirp chirp

Fish: swim swim   Horse: neigh neigh

Lamb: baa baa   Duck: quack quack

Song

What You Need
- duplicated page

What To Do
1. Sing the song to the tune of "Old MacDonald."
2. Use the extra pet words to sing more verses to the song.
3. Older babies will enjoy helping you make the animal sounds.

My Pets

Learning Play

What You Need
- this page, duplicated
- plastic laundry detergent lids, 6 or more, in a variety of bright colors
- glue
- scissors

What To Do
1. Before class, cut the six circles from the pattern page. You may use more than one pattern page for this game if you wish. Glue one animal circle to the top, flat end of each detergent lid.
2. To play the game, put all the game pieces with the picture sides down. Help each baby choose a game piece and look at the animal picture. Say, **Peek-a-boo, we found a kitty. Let's see what other pets we can find. We give thanks to God for our pets.**

Peek-a-Boo Pets

My Pets

Indoor/Outdoor Pets Book

Indoor/Outdoor Pets

My Pets

Read to Me

What You Need
- duplicated pages 43, 44 and 45
- construction paper
- glue
- hole punch
- plastic rings

What To Do

1. Before class, glue the cover page (page 43) to a piece of construction paper. Place pages 44 and 45 (second and third pages of activity) inside two pieces of construction paper. Punch holes along the left side of the book. Place three plastic rings through the holes to hold the book together.
2. Hold each baby and read the rhymes out loud. Let older babies point to the animals to try to guess which one is an indoor or outdoor pet.
3. Say, **We thank God for all our indoor and outdoor pets.**

I have a pet,

He lives indoors.

He sometimes meows

But he never roars.

I have a pet

With a soft, fluffy head.

She sleeps in a barn

Not in my bed.

I have a pet,

He lives outside.

He can't sit on my lap

But on his back I can ride.

I have a pet,

She likes to play.

I keep her on a leash

When we walk outdoors each day.

Hands On

What You Need
- duplicated page
- cardboard tubes
- yarn
- glue
- crayons
- scissors
- tape

What To Do
1. Before class, cut out the four pet shapes from the pattern page. Glue one shape to the side of each of four cardboard tubes. Cut a one-yard or longer length of yarn and thread it through all four tubes. Tape each tube at intervals along the yarn. Leave a few inches at the front of the first tube as a handle.
2. Help each baby pull the Pet Parade along the floor. Say, **Look at our pretty pets. We can take our pets for a walk. We give thanks to God for our pets.**
3. Older babies may enjoy scribble-coloring the animals on the tubes.

My Pets

Pet Parade

finished craft

Hiding Lamb

finished craft

Learning Play

What You Need
- duplicated page
- plastic convenience store soda cup, 32 ounce or larger
- glue
- scissors

What To Do
1. Before class, cut the lamb face from the pattern page. Glue the face to the flat bottom end of the plastic cup. Glue cotton balls on the sides of the cup to look like a lamb.
2. Show each baby the lamb. Then, "hide" the lamb under a baby's blanket, or under a chair, on highchair seat, etc. Help each baby find the lamb. Say, **The man in our Bible story couldn't find his little lamb. He looked and looked. Finally, he said, "I am very happy. I have found my lost lamb."** We give thanks to God for lambs and other pets.

My Pets

Chapter 5
Thank You God For Food

Memory Verse

Ravens brought [Elijah] bread and meat.
~I Kings 17:6

Story to Share

Elijah was a special messenger from God. Elijah told God's people that God would send no rain for a long time. Without rain, there would be no water to drink and no food to eat.

God told Elijah to go to a special place and sit by a brook that would always have water for Elijah. God also said, "I have told the ravens to bring you food there."

So Elijah went where God told him. He had plenty of water. And the ravens brought him bread and meat two times every day. Elijah had good food for breakfast and for supper.

God provided Elijah with good food to eat. God provides us with good food to eat, too.

~Based on I Kings 17:1-6

Story Review

1. What did Elijah say to the people about rain? Elijah said that God would send no rain for a long time.

2. How did God take care of Elijah? God told Elijah to go stay in a special place by a brook. Elijah would have water there. God also told the ravens to bring Elijah bread and meat two times every day.

 ## Parent Corner

1. *Feeding time sharing.* At feeding time, show your baby the story poster. Tell the story while the baby looks at the poster. Ask and answer the discussion questions on the page. Repeat the story, memory verse or lesson theme several times while feeding your child.

2. While shopping for groceries, let your baby hold some safe items. Say, **God gives us good food to eat. We like to eat carrots. We give thanks to God for good food.**

3. If you have not already begun to teach your baby to pray at meals, now is a great time to start. Even if your child is nursing or taking a bottle, get in the habit of helping your baby fold his/her hands to thank God for good food. At the table, let your baby see the entire family thanking God for food.

Bulletin Board

What You Need
- pattern on page 51
- clear adhesive-backed plastic
- magazine pictures of food
- glue

What To Do
1. Depending on how you want to use the poster (see ideas below), enlarge, reduce or simply copy page 51 to fit your bulletin board space.
2. To make a take-home paper, duplicate the story page on the back of the story poster.

Food

❧ Story Poster ❧

⟶ Poster Pointer

To use the poster as an in-class activity, turn the poster over and help children glue some pictures of foods they like onto the page.

Learning Play

What You Need
- pages 52 and 53 duplicated, two copies of each
- Twelve paper or plastic plates, any size
- scissors
- glue

What To Do
1. Before class, cut out two sets of the six circles. Glue one on the inside of each of the twelve paper or plastic plates.
2. To play the game, place all the plates upside down on a table or play mat.
3. Help each baby pick up two plates. Turn the plates over and see if the food items match. Say, **Jackson found a banana and an apple. God made good food to eat.** If the baby matches two food items, help them clap their hands.
4. For younger babies, simply hold one of the plates and let them touch the picture. Say, **Thank you God for food.**

Food

Large Matching Game

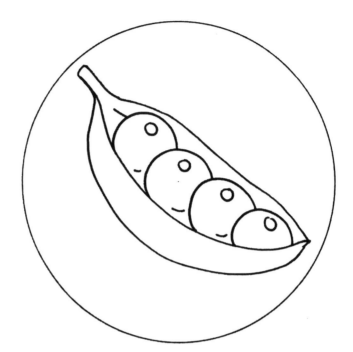

finished craft

Hands-On

What You Need
- pages 54 and 55, duplicated
- felt piece for each child's food stickers
- scissors
- glue
- tape

What To Do
1. Before class, cut out the bib pattern. Use the pattern to trace and cut a bib from felt for each child. Cut out the food shapes from the second page. Glue food shapes to each bib. Let the glue dry before using the project with children.
2. Let babies touch the bibs. Use for snack or feeding time, or just to retell the story. Babies will enjoy touching the pictures on the bibs.
3. Help babies fold their hands and thank God for good food.

Food

Thank You Bibs

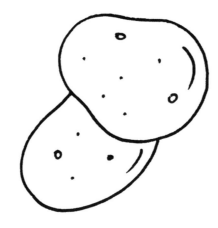
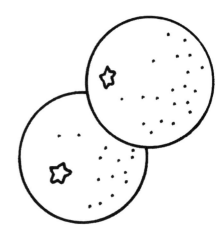
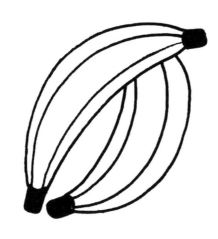
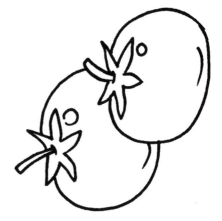

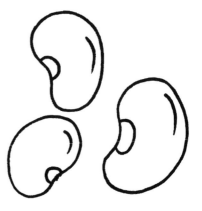

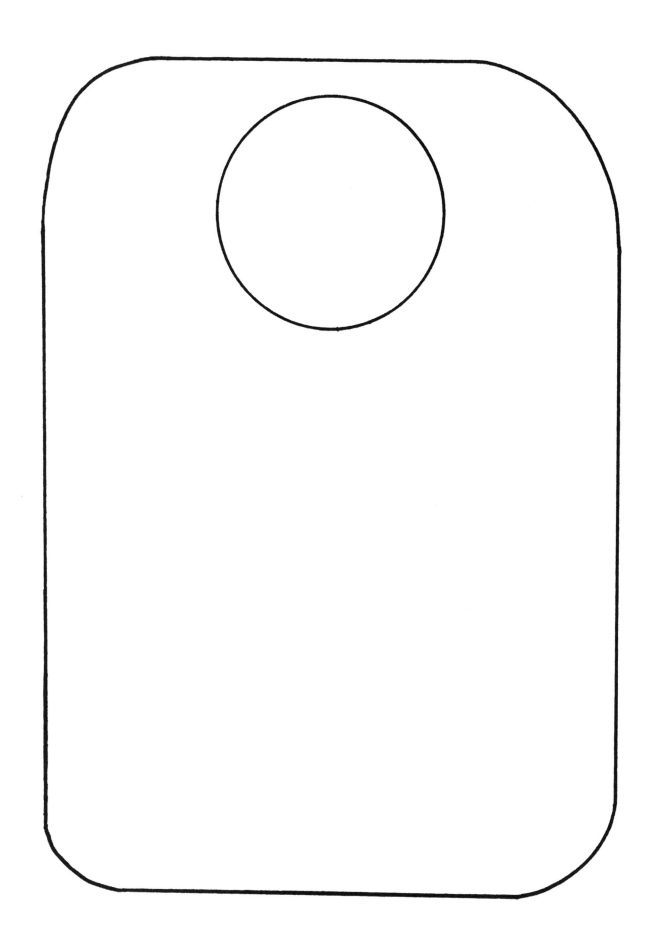

Song

What You Need
- duplicated page

What To Do
1. Sing the song, "God Gave Us Good Food," to the tune of "Ten Little Indians."
2. For older babies, sing extra verses to the song. Substitute the name of a food in place of the words "good food."
3. Older babies can point to the picture of each food while you sing the song together. Encourage each baby to sing along.

Food

God Gave Us Good Food

God gave us food, gave us good food to eat,
God gave us food, gave us good food to eat,
God gave us food, gave us good food to eat,
Thank you God for good food.

➡ **Words to Substitute for extra verses:**

Bananas
Potatoes
Beans
Tomatoes
Oranges
Apples

Thanking God Action Rhyme

I fold my hands and pray to God.
I thank him for my food.

I love to say, "Thank you God,"
For food that tastes so good.

Rhyme

What You Need
- duplicated page

What To Do
1. Say the rhyme at least once, doing the actions.
2. Say the rhyme again, helping baby make praying hands.

Food

Praying Hands

Easy Craft

What You Need
- duplicated page for each child
- crayons
- tape
- yarn

What To Do
1. Before class, cut out the prayer rectangle and an 8-inch length of yarn for each child.
2. Help children fold the praying hands rectangle in half.
3. Older babies will enjoy scribble-coloring the pictures of praying hands.
4. Tape a loop of yarn to top of craft.
5. Say, **This is what our hands look like when we pray to God.** Help babies form their own praying hands.

Food

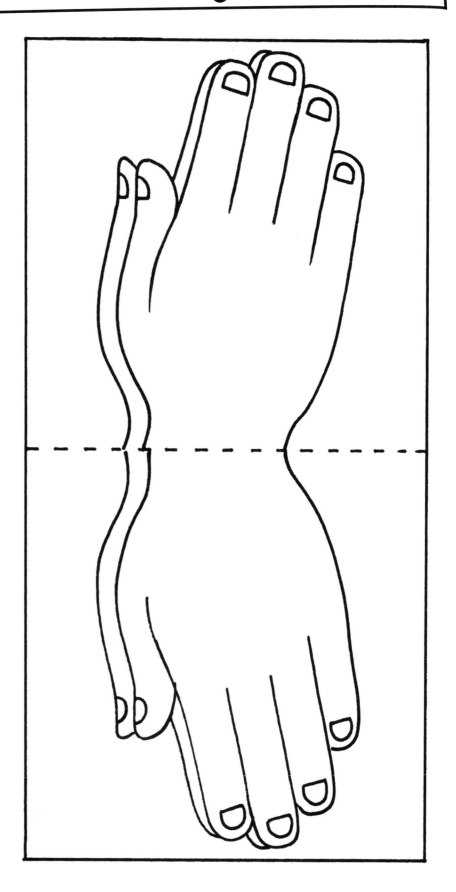

58

Praying Hands Puzzle

God, You are kind.
God, You are good.
We thank You God.

Puzzle

What You Need
- duplicated page for each child
- crayons

What To Do
1. Read the prayer to each baby or group of babies.
2. Help each baby hold a crayon and color each of the two hidden praying hands.
3. Say, **The boy and girl are praying to thank God for their food. Let's color the two praying hands hidden in the picture.**

Food

Chapter 6
Thank You God for water

Memory Verse

You will bring water out of the rock.
~Numbers 20:8

Story to Share

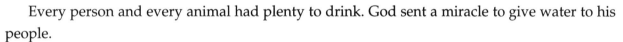

God's people were traveling through the wilderness, just as God had planned for them to do. But the people couldn't find any water to drink. They told Moses and Aaron, "We need water to drink. Our children need water. Our animals need water. What will we do?"

God told Moses to gather all the people together around a big rock. Then Moses raised his arms. He did just as God told him to do. Moses struck the big rock with his staff. Then water began to pour from the rock.

Every person and every animal had plenty to drink. God sent a miracle to give water to his people.

God provides all we need. We give thanks to God for water.

~Based on Numbers 20:1-11

Story Review

1. Who did God's people tell that they wanted water? God's people told Moses and Aaron.

2. Who helped the people have water? God did a miracle and provided water.

3. Where did the water come from? The water came from a rock.

Parent Corner

1. Make use of waiting time. When you are waiting in a doctor's office, a lobby or even a long line at the super market, tell the story to your baby. This will help keep him/her from becoming restless and fussy, as well as reinforcing the Bible truth once again.

2. Let your baby see you pour water into his/her bottle or sippy cup. Say, **God gives us water. We give thanks to God for water.**

3. As you go about daily chores, speak to your baby about each time you use water. Mention different situations in which you use water.

Bulletin Board

What You Need
- pattern on page 63
- clear adhesive-backed plastic
- pretzel sticks
- gray felt
- blue gel icing
- glue

What To Do
1. Depending on how you want to use the poster (see ideas below), enlarge, reduce or simply copy page 63 to fit your bulletin board space.
2. To make a take-home paper, duplicate the story page to the back of story poster.
3. To use the poster as an in-class activity, add texture items to the picture. Glue a pretzel stick to Moses' staff and a piece of felt to the rock. Squeeze blue gel icing on the water coming from the rock.

water

Story Poster

▬▶ Poster Pointer

Attach poster to brightly colored paper. Fasten the poster to the bulletin board. Carry children to the bulletin board several times during class time. Say the memory verse or retell the story while you help child touch the story poster.

Song

What You Need
- duplicated page
- cotton swabs
- cups of water tinted slightly with blue food coloring

What To Do
1. Sing the song with children to the tune of "London Bridge." Do the actions to the song.
2. Help children do the actions while you sing the song again.
3. Help older babies use the cotton swabs and blue water to paint the poster picture blue. Say, **God gives us water.**

water

God Gives Us Water

God sent water from a rock
[touch chest with both hands and sweep hands out like gushing water]

From a rock

From a rock

God sent water from a rock
[sweep hands out like gushing water]

For His people.

God sends rain to give us water
[wiggle fingers like falling rain]

Give us water

Give us water

God sends rain to give us water.
[wiggle fingers like falling rain]

Thank you, God.
[fold hands in prayer]

Thankful for Water Cup

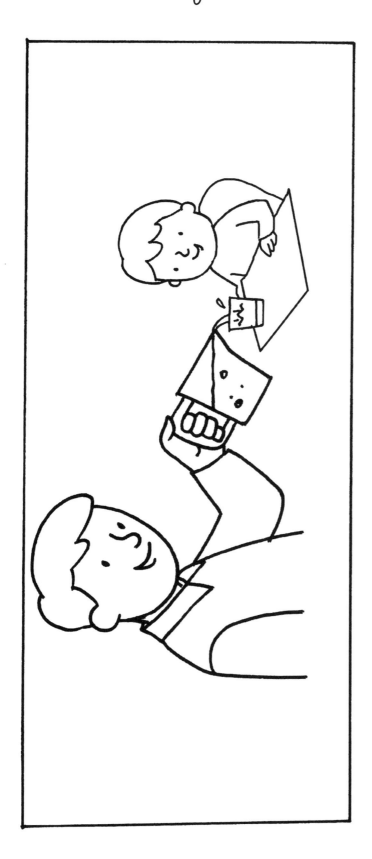

Easy Craft

What You Need
- duplicated page
- clear adhesive-backed plastic
- plastic cups
- crayons
- scissors
- tape

What To Do
1. Before class, cut out a paper strip from the pattern page for each child.
2. Help older babies scribble-color the picture strip.
3. Tape the paper strip to the cup, then place the plastic protective covering over the paper strip.
4. Let babies see you pour water into at least one cup. Offer older babies a drink of water from the cup they made. Say, **We give thanks to God for water.**

water

Water Rhymes Booklet

Read to Me

What You Need
- duplicated page for each child
- crayons

What To Do
1. Before class, fold the pattern page into quarters to form a book for each child.
2. Read the rhymes to the children. Thank God together for water.
3. Older babies may want to scribble-color their booklets.

Water Wheel Game

Learning Play

What You Need
- page duplicated to card stock
- paper fastener
- scissors
- plastic cup
- bar of soap (in wrapper)
- flower in a pot
- toy car

What To Do
1. Before class, cut the water wheel circle and spinner needle from the pattern page. Push a paper fastener through X on the needle and the water wheel. Make loose enough to turn easily.
2. Set these items on the table next to the water wheel: cup, bar of soap, flower in a pot, toy car.
3. To play the game, have each baby turn the needle to a picture. For older babies, say, **Which of these things match the picture? Daddy is washing the car.**
4. For younger babies, turn the wheel and pick up each item for the baby. Thank God for water.

water

Puzzle

What You Need
- duplicated page for each child
- crayons

What To Do
1. Help each baby hold the puzzle page.
2. Say, **Let's find some things we do with water. Who is getting a drink of water? Yes, the baby, the dog and the horse are getting a drink of water. Who is having a bath? Yes, the bird, the baby and the dog are having a bath.**
3. Older babies can scribble color or put a mark on the scenes as you discuss each one.

water

Things We Do with Water Puzzle

water Shakers

Learning Play

what You Need
- duplicated page
- small jars with lids
- water
- food coloring
- liquid soap
- glitter
- scissors
- tape

what To Do
1. Before class, cut out the three circles. Glue one circle to the top of each lid.
2. Fill the three bottles halfway with water. Add the following items, one to each bottle: liquid soap, glitter, food coloring. Place the lids on the bottles tightly.
3. Let each baby shake the bottles. Say, **This bottle makes pretty colors with water. This bottle makes bubbles with water. See the glitter in this bottle of water? We give thanks to God for water.**

water

Chapter 7
Thank You God for Clothes

Memory Verse
[Jacob] made a robe for [Joseph].
~Genesis 37:3

Story to Share

Jacob loved his little boy Joseph very much. Jacob gave Joseph a beautiful coat of many colors to wear because he was so proud of his son. Joseph was thankful for his beautiful coat.

God loves us very much. God gives us the things we need.

We give thanks to God for our clothes.

~Based on Genesis 37:1-11

Story Review

1. What did Jacob give to Joseph? Jacob gave Joseph a beautiful coat to wear.

2. Who gives us things we need to have clothes to wear? God gives us the things we need to have clothes to wear.

Parent Corner

1. Bedtime storytelling. Pat your baby's arm or shoulder while telling the Bible story in a soothing voice. Retell the story until your child falls asleep.

2. Talk about clothes while you dress your baby. Say, **This is a pretty blue shirt. God helps us have the clothes we wear. Thank you, God.**

3. Let older babies put some of his/her clothing on a baby doll. Say, **What a good job you are doing dressing the baby. God gives us our clothes. We give thanks to God for our clothes.**

Bulletin Board

What You Need
- pattern on page 73
- clear adhesive-backed plastic
- paint sample strips from a paint store
- glue

What To Do
1. Depending on how you want to use the poster (see ideas below), enlarge, reduce, or simply copy page 73 to fit your bulletin board space.
2. To make a take-home paper, duplicate the story page to the back of story poster.
3. To use the poster as an in-class activity, help children glue a paint sample strip (with several shades of one color), onto Joseph's coat in the picture.

Clothes

Story Poster

Poster Pointer

Use a thumb tack to fasten a plastic page protector pocket onto the wall just outside your nursery room door. Each week, slip the story poster inside the pocket so parents will see what their child is learning in nursery.

Hands On

What You Need
- duplicated pages 74 and 75
- clear adhesive-backed plastic
- scissors

What To Do
1. Before class, cut out the paper doll from this page. Cut out the two outfits from page 75. Cover the paper doll and the two outfits with clear adhesive-backed plastic.
2. Help each baby place one of the extra outfits on the paper doll. Say, **What pretty clothes we can put on the child. We give thanks to God for clothes.**

Clothes

Play Clothes Paper Doll

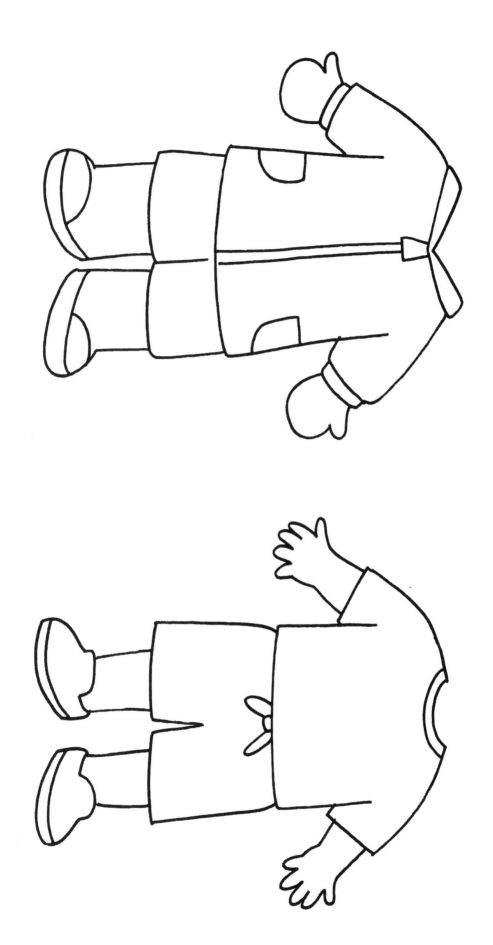

Song

What You Need
- duplicated page
- red, green and blue crayons

What To Do
1. Before class, color the shirts on the page, one red, one green, one blue.
2. Sing the song to the tune of "Itsy Bitsy Spider." Point to the colors as you say them.
3. After singing the song, help the children fold hands in prayer to thank God for our clothes.

What Shall I Wear?

What color shall I wear

when I go out to play?

Will it be blue, green or red,

which one would you say?

I think I'll wear my favorite,

that is what I'll do.

I have a favorite color to wear,

how about you?

Clothes

Coat of Many Colors Mobile

finished craft

Room Decoration

What You Need
- duplicated page for each mobile
- baby-sized clothes hanger for each mobile
- crepe paper streamers, 4 colors
- scissors
- tape

What To Do
1. Before class, cut out the Joseph figures from this page. Tape the Joseph figure onto the clothes hanger, with the head of Joseph covering the hook of the hanger.
2. Tape 1-foot lengths of crepe paper onto each mobile. Use four different colors for each mobile.
3. Hang the mobiles around the room. Lift babies so they can touch the pretty mobiles. Say, **What a pretty coat Joseph has. We give thanks to God for our clothes.**

Clothes

Puzzle

What You Need
- duplicated page, two copies
- craft foam
- scissors

What To Do
1. Before class, cut clothing items out from one duplicated page. Trace the shirt and pants onto craft foam and cut out two or more of each. Use a variety of colors.
2. Have the children help you place the craft foam shirt and pants on the child in the puzzle. Say, **Which color shirt shall we put on the baby? Oh, yellow is very pretty. We give thanks to God for our clothes.**
3. Each baby can place different colors of clothes on the child in the puzzle.

Clothes

My Clothes Puzzle

✳ Mosaic Verse Poster ✳

Many colors
Many colors
Joseph's new coat was many colors
Thank you God for Joseph's new coat.

Many colors
Many colors
I have clothes that are many colors.
Thank you God for my clothes.

Easy Craft

What You Need
- duplicated page for each child
- glue sticks
- construction paper

What To Do
1. Before class, cut several squares (around 1 inch) from construction paper.
2. Place the rhyme poster on the table. Spread several colors of squares around the poster.
3. Say the rhyme with the children.
4. Help the children glue some colorful squares inside the blank squares on the poster page.
5. Say, **Our clothes are many colors, just like Joseph's coat. We give thanks to God for our clothes.**

Clothes

Story in a Diaper Bag

Read to Me

What You Need
- duplicated page
- diaper bag with the following items inside: diaper, socks, shoes, shirt, pants, pajamas

What To Do
1. Before class, put the baby items in a diaper bag. If you do not have the items, ask one of the nursery parents to provide the items for you.
2. Read the story to the children. Each time you say one of the picture-words, show that item from the diaper bag.
3. For more one-on-one time with older babies, let the child reach into the diaper bag and get an item. Pretend to put that item on the baby. Say, **We give thanks to God for our shoes and socks.**

Socks   Shoes   Shirt   Pants   Pajamas

Grandma picked up Davy. "You are still wearing your [pajamas]. I think we should get you dressed and go for a walk in the park."

Grandma took a blue [shirt] from Davy's closet. "What a pretty blue [shirt]," she said.

Grandma opened Davy's dresser drawer and found some gray [pants]. "I like these gray [pants]," she told Davy.

"Let's take off those [pajamas]." Grandma let Davy sit on Mommy's big bed. She took off Davy's [pajamas]. "Oh, I see a tummy!" Davy giggled when Grandma tickled his tummy.

"Now," Grandma said, "put on your gray [pants]. Lift up your arms and we'll put on your blue [shirt].

Grandma put one [sock] on the left foot and one [sock] on the right foot. "Now we can put on your [shoes]." She put one [shoe] on Davy's left foot. Then she put the other [shoe] on Davy's right foot.

"You are all dressed now." Grandma said. "We are all ready to go for a walk in the park!"

Chapter 8
Thank You God for My Church

Memory Verse

Every day they [met] with glad hearts.
~Acts 2:46

 Story to Share

Jesus' followers worked hard to tell people about Jesus. They taught people about Jesus and God. The people who heard about Jesus and God became part of God's family.

More and more people learned about God and became part of His family. The people met together every day to learn about God and to praise Him. Everyone shared with each other. They showed great love for each other.

Our church is just like the first churches in the Bible. We meet together to learn and to praise God. We are all part of God's family. We share with each other. We show love for each other. We give thanks to God for our church.

~Based on Acts 2:42-47

Story Review

1. Whose family did the people become part of? The people learned about God and became part of God's family.

2. Whose family are we part of when we believe in God? We are part of God's family, too.

3. What can we do to show we are part of God's family? We can come to church to learn about God. We can share with each other. We can show love for each other.

Parent Corner

1. *Together Coloring Time.* Sit at a table with your baby. Place the story poster on the table. Help him/her hold a crayon and scribble-color the story poster. Tell the story while your baby is coloring.

2. Take some canned goods to the church or a local food pantry. Say to your baby, **We are sharing with others because we are part of God's family.**

3. Pick your baby up from nursery a little early next week. Let him/her be with you when you talk and share with other church members. Say, **We are all part of God's family. We can show love for each other.**

Bulletin Board

What You Need
- pattern on page 83
- clear adhesive-backed plastic
- toy dollar bills
- glue or tape
- small cutout pictures of food and clothing

What To Do
1. Depending on how you want to use the poster, enlarge, reduce or simply copy page 83 to fit your space.
2. To make a take-home paper, duplicate the story page to the back of story poster.
3. To use the poster as an in-class activity, help the children glue toy dollar bills and pictures of food and clothing to the picture. Say, **The church shared their money, food, clothes and everything they had with each other. Our church shares and shows love for each other, too. We give thanks to God for our church.**

My Church

Story Poster

Poster Pointer

Copy the poster for each lesson in this book to card stock. You may laminate the pages with clear adhesive-backed plastic, if you wish. Place the eight posters together. Punch the left edge with a three-ring hole punch. Fasten the book together with plastic rings or loose strands of yarn in the three holes on the left edge. Use the book as a read-to-me activity for rocking-chair time or playtime.

Every day they [met] with glad hearts.

~Acts 2:46

Learning Play

What You Need
- duplicated page
- offering tray
- scissors
- envelopes
- crayons

What To Do
1. Before class, cut out the shapes from the page.
2. Lay the money shapes on the table, next to an offering tray.
3. Let the children put the money into the tray.
4. Say, **We can give our money to share with our church. We give thanks to God for our church.**
5. Optional: cut out the money shapes for each child, or at least the older babies. Let them help you place the money inside an envelope. Write on the outside of the envelope, **We can give our money to share with our church.** Let each baby take home the envelope to do the activity with their parents.

My Church

Offering Tray Game

My Church

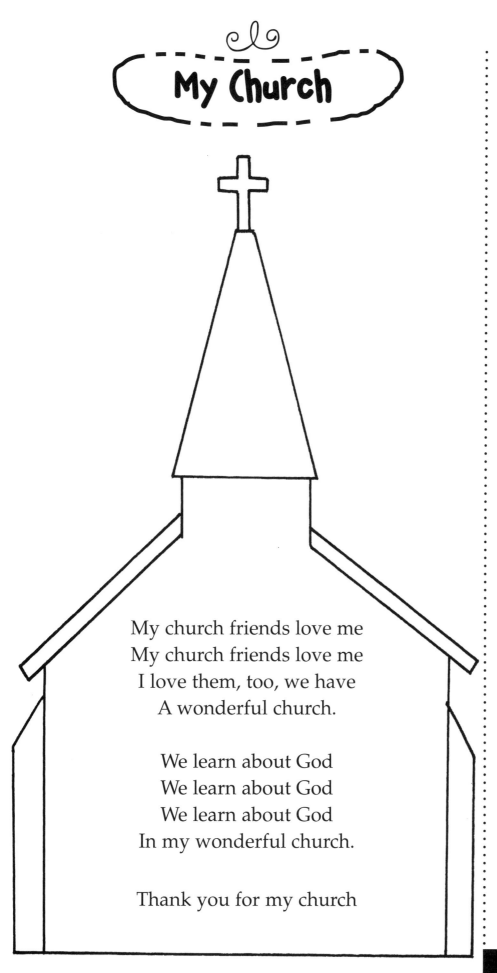

My church friends love me
My church friends love me
I love them, too, we have
A wonderful church.

We learn about God
We learn about God
We learn about God
In my wonderful church.

Thank you for my church

Song

What You Need
- duplicated page
- cotton swabs
- glue

What To Do
1. Sing the song "My Church" to the tune of "God Is So Good."
2. Let the children touch the picture of the church while you sing the song again with them.
3. Older babies will enjoy outlining the church shape by gluing on cotton swabs.

My Church

Rhyme

What You Need
- duplicated page
- crayons

What To Do
1. Say the verses while helping the children fold their hands to make the actions.
2. For older babies, say the third verse together a few times in order to replace the word "friend" for each child's name.
3. Babies may enjoy scribble-coloring the picture to take home. Parents can do the activity at home with children to reinforce the lesson.

My Church

I Can Make a Church

I put my hands together to make a roof
[put finger tips together to form a roof]
make a roof
make a roof
I put my hands together
to make a roof

I put the roof over my head
[put finger tips together and hold hands over head]
over my head
over my head
I put the roof over my head
I am inside the church

I put the roof over my friend's head
[put finger tips together and hold hands over a friend's head]
She [he] is inside the church
She [he] is inside the church
I put the roof over my friend's head
She [he] is inside the church

Sharing Bank

Option
You may want to discuss the bank with parents when they pick up their children. Decide together on a worthy project inside the church building or in the community to use the money to help.

Easy Craft

What You Need
- duplicated page, one for every two children
- plastic square baby wipe containers
- scissors
- glue
- crayons

What To Do
1. Before class, cut out the church picture from the pattern page, one per child. Cut a hole in the top of the plastic baby wipe container, large enough to fit coins through.
2. Help baby color the church (if desired) and glue the church shape to one side of the wipe container.
3. Say, **We are making a sharing bank. You can take the bank home and put money inside. When the bank is filled, you can bring the money to share in the offering.**

My Church

Puzzle

Meet Together with Gladness Puzzle

What You Need
- page duplicated to card stock
- scissors

What To Do
1. Before class, cut the puzzle apart on the marked lines.
2. Help the children assemble the puzzle.
3. Say, **The first church met together with gladness. Our church meets together with gladness, too.**

My Church

Chapter 9
More Give Thanks to God Activities

Clapping Rhyme

Clap your hands (and help babies clap) in rhythm to the following rhyme. Say at least the first verse.

Thank you, God
Thank you, God
I just like to say,
Thank you, God.

▶ Optional:

Substitute the third line for the following lines for older babies to reinforce each lesson:

For my family	For my friends
For my home	For my pets
For good food	For our water
For my clothes	For my church

Thank You Praying Toy

Hands On

What You Need
- duplicated page
- two plastic plates
- scrap of craft foam
- paper fasteners
- glue
- tape

What To Do
1. Before class, cut the two clock circles from the pattern page. Glue each clock to the backside center of the plastic plate. Cut two arrows, about 3 inches wide and 1 inch tall from craft foam scraps. Use paper fasteners to attach one arrow to the center of each clock in the marked X. Tape the plates together securely, with the clock side facing out.
2. While holding each child, turn the arrow to one of the pictures on the clock. Read the phrase and let the child touch the picture. Turn the clock over so the baby can see both sides of the clock and hear you thank God for each of the eight themes.

More

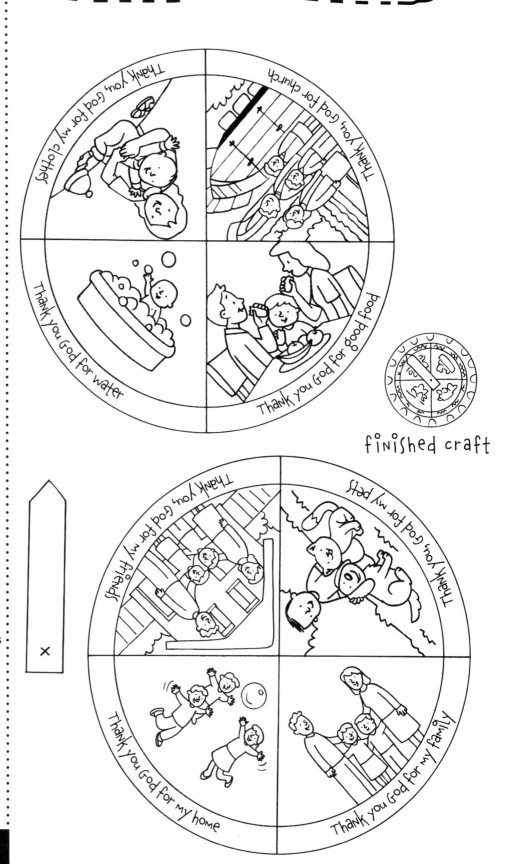

finished craft

Glow-in-the-Dark Praying Hands Plaque

Easy Craft

What You Need
- page duplicated to card stock for each child
- scissors
- yarn
- tape
- glow in the dark glitter
- crayons
- glue

What To Do
1. Before class, cut out an oval plaque for each child. Tape a loop of yarn to the top of each plaque for a hanger.
2. Older babies may enjoy scribble-coloring the praying hands picture.
3. Help babies spread some glow-in-the-dark glitter around the edge of the plaque or outline the praying hands, as you wish.
4. Help the babies fold their hands. Say, **See the picture. This is how our hands look when we are praying to God. We pray to thank God for all the good things He gives us.**

More

Beanbag Toss Game

Learning Play

What You Need
- this page duplicated to plain paper
- pages 93 and 94, duplicated to card stock
- scissors
- tape
- paper scraps for stuffing

What To Do
1. Before class, cut the beanbag rectangle from the page. Fold the rectangle in half. Tape two sides securely. Stuff the beanbag with paper scraps. Tape the edge securely. Tape the two "game board" pages together.
2. Place the game board on a table or play mat.
3. Give baby the beanbag to toss onto the game board.
4. Say, **Kate has thrown her beanbag on a picture of a kitten. We give thanks to God for our special pets.**
5. Continue to play with one or more babies at a time, depending on helpers and how long you can get the children to enjoy the game.

More

Praying Hands

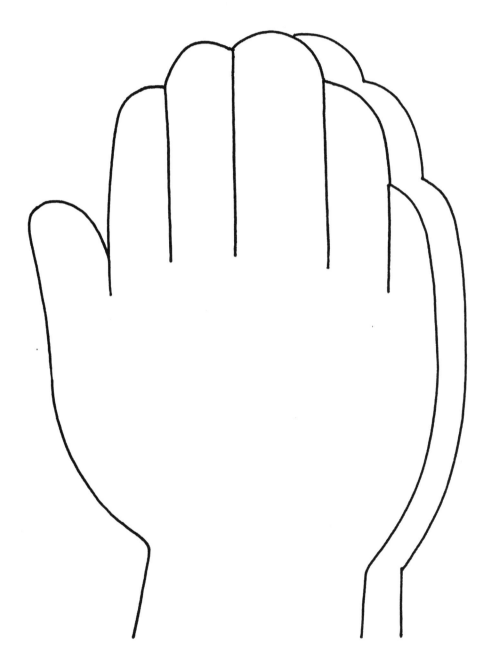

Room Decoration

What You Need
- page duplicated to transparency sheets
- scissors
- fishing line
- tape
- permanent markers

What To Do
1. Before class, cut out the praying hands shapes. For a hanger, tape a length of fishing line to the top edge of each praying hands.
2. As you work with babies during class time, trace each baby's hand onto one of the praying hands shapes. Write the baby's name on the praying hands.
3. Hang the praying hands around the room. Let each child see the one with their name on it. Say, **This says, "Elizabeth." Elizabeth can pray and thank God for all the good things He gives us.**

More

Rattling Roller Game

Learning Play

What You Need
- duplicated page
- round oatmeal box with lid, any size
- dried beans or jingle bells
- tape
- scissors

What To Do
1. Before class, cut the two strips from the pattern page. Tape the strips onto the oatmeal box. Depending on the size of the box, you may tape the strips in a continuous circle around the box, or one just above the other, wherever they fit best on the box. Place some dried beans or jingle bells inside the oatmeal box. Tape the lid securely onto the box.
2. While sitting on a play mat with the children, roll the round box to each child. Babies will love the sound it makes. Roll the box back and forth a few times.

More

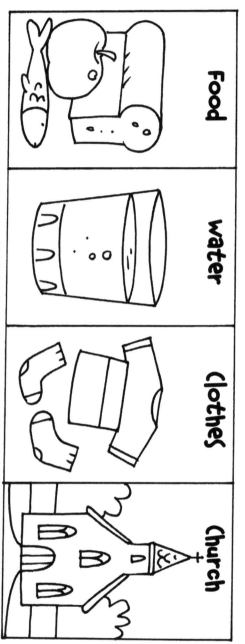

What To Do, continued...
3. Each time a baby touches the box, say, **This is our thank-you box. We thank God for our family.** (Say each item that is on the strip around the box)